Contents

In our neighbourhood

A regional theatre and its local community

A report on a developing relationship between

The West Yorkshire Playhouse
& Ebor Gardens Estate, Leeds

Dick Downing

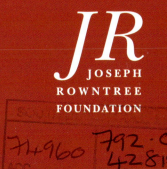

JR
JOSEPH
ROWNTREE
FOUNDATION

The Joseph Rowntree Foundation has supported this project as part of its programme of research and development projects, which it hopes will be of value to policy makers, practitioners and service users. The facts presented and views expressed in this report, however, are those of the author and not necessarily those of the Foundation.

All photographs by Simon Warner except pages 16 and 41 by Keith Pattison

Published by
Joseph Rowntree Foundation
The Homestead
40 Water End
York
YO30 6WP
www.jrf.org.uk

ISBN 1 85935 064 X

Price £13.95

Designed by Epigram
Printed by Stott Brothers Ltd

Printed on recycled paper

Foreword

I suppose much of what I write for the theatre and TV is about people succeeding over adversity, finding confidence knowing they have the support of their community and family. As a Leeds playwright and board member of the West Yorkshire Playhouse, it pleases me no end to see a diverse bunch of people in both our auditoriums. When the Playhouse first opened, it was part of our policy to actively encourage a wider audience and serve the community. It was the Playhouse's mission to get to know what the local communities wanted and encourage them to be actively involved. Hence the eclectic mix of plays that we produce and the variety of activities ranging from pre-school to the over-subscribed Heydays (for over-55s) – try finding an empty room in the Playhouse any day of the week!

As well as their everyday policy, the Playhouse initiated a specific year-long intensive community project called 'In our neighbourhood', which was to develop a creative relationship with a neighbouring estate – Ebor Gardens. It resulted in a rewarding two-way learning curve for both parties. The Playhouse learnt more about what their local community actually wanted and the community learnt that 'next door' at the theatre, there wasn't just a bunch of archaic, theatre luvvies, bedecked in feather boas, but a rich experience just waiting to be had.

The community is at the heart of theatre, the two are intrinsically linked. Historically, it is how we communicate. To laugh, learn, to be affronted, intrigued, frightened, moved to tears, together with others, only heightens the experience and surely everyone should have the opportunity of that experience.

Kay Mellor
Writer, director and actor

During 1999 and 2000, the West Yorkshire Playhouse in Leeds undertook a programme of work to explore the possibility of making itself more accessible to its most local residential community, the Ebor Gardens Estate. It was supported by the Joseph Rowntree Foundation, and the project was called 'In our neighbourhood'.

Over a period of twelve months the Playhouse targeted the work of a number of their staff on this neighbouring estate. The objectives of the project were: to increase the range and quality of what the Playhouse offers the community; to increase the take-up by the community of new and existing WYP services and products, through improved accessibility; and to increase the awareness and commitment of the WYP institution and staff to supporting the needs and aspirations of the local community. During the short time of the project, the Playhouse established a relationship with the community that produced some surprising results.

The project found that:

- Providing one-to-one advice and support to key individuals on the estate was a central strategy in cementing the relationship.

- Workers on the estate, both paid and voluntary, were an important source of advice concerning the style and content of the project.

- Staff from the theatre became part of a broader support network and forged strong bonds with estate residents.

- Although residents were initially keen to see a developing programme of participatory activities, in practice there was reluctance to engage in them, for a variety of reasons including a lack of confidence and in some cases a preference to continue with their already existing creative activities. It is possible that these barriers could have been overcome over a longer time scale.

- The project developed in fits and starts. A laid-back approach was found to be more productive than a high-energy 'intervention'.

- The project produced many good things for residents on the estate, for community workers and for the community centre:
  - there was increased communication between residents, partly due to a new shared interest;
  - residents supported each other more actively;
  - some residents developed the confidence to plan ahead for social activities, such as a visit to the theatre, rather than feeling that they could not see beyond one day at a time;
  - the partnership helped community workers on the estate by supporting their on-going work and stimulating residents' interest in community based projects;
  - the project stimulated more and wider usage of the community centre (which was used as a 'box office' during the project).

- During the time of the project, mainstream theatre attendance increased at a startling rate. This was one of the most unexpected and successful outcomes, and indicates an interest in attending the theatre amongst residents that had not previously been acted upon.

- Local residents found it much easier to relate to their neighbouring institution through encountering its staff in person, than through standard publicity material.

- The assumption held by residents that they would not be welcome in the theatre and the assumption held by the theatre that the residents would want something other than mainstream theatre experiences, have both been undermined.

- Many departments from the theatre, not simply the community department itself, became involved in the new relationship with the community.

Part I

The context

chapter 1

Introduction

For many people in Britain, theatre is already a significant element in their cultural lives. There has been considerable concern about the financial viability of many of our regional theatres in recent years, and central government, through the Arts Council of England, is about to inject additional funding in recognition of and support for the part that theatre can play in community, social and educational development.

However, theatre traditionally has been attended in large part by a small minority of the population as a whole, in spite of the strenuous effort of theatre practitioners who have been committed to 'social inclusion' since long before the term became a political buzz-word. Too often characterised as middle class and middle aged, theatre audiences have been changing, and have always been changing. But this does not mean that theatres can simply rest on their box office figures, however successful they may be. When public subsidy is keeping them afloat, they need to ensure that the widest possible cross-section of the community benefits from the investment.

This report examines a substantial experiment in partnership working between two neighbours, the West Yorkshire Playhouse (WYP) and the Ebor Gardens Estate in Leeds. At their closest point, they are no more than three hundred yards apart, as the crow flies. Both have experienced a form of rebirth during the last decade of the twentieth century. Like any theatre, or any estate, they have unique characteristics, while sharing with theatres and estates around the country a large number of common features.

Unlike more conventional community arts projects, 'In our neighbourhood' was initiated by a large, mainstream, thriving arts institution, who, as sole applicants, approached the Joseph Rowntree Foundation (JRF) for assistance in setting up a project to work with their local community. No one from the local community was involved at this stage in the application, even though the project was intended to 'create an innovative model for a relationship between an arts institution and a neighbourhood'.[1] The use of the word 'relationship' might usually imply a willingness, or at least interest, in each party to pursue such a 'relationship', but a two-sided interest was yet to be established.

This anomaly reflects to a degree the challenge facing the arts in relationship to the population as a whole. Unlike the process of marketing more tangible consumer products, the arts defy description or definition: to know fully in advance what one was buying would often render the product worthless. It is the delight of risk or surprise, which is the main attraction. Only practice in this peculiar type of risk-taking, established over a period of time, enables participants to enter into and enjoy that 'relationship'.

Small wonder, then, that only about 23 per cent of the population of this country enter into such 'blind dates' with the subsidised arts on anything like a regular basis. The risk being proposed by the West Yorkshire Playhouse, and accepted by the Joseph Rowntree Foundation, was therefore to see if a particular sector of the population could, over a relatively short period of time, be drawn into such a relationship, thus overcoming a particular form of social exclusion.

One might argue that a kind of arrogance on the part of the WYP allowed them to pursue such a course. Why presume that the neighbours should want to become involved in this relationship? Wasn't their success with other groups within the Leeds population sufficient for them? Could it be that not everyone in this society needs or wants to have an involvement with the subsidised arts?

Complex issues arise from such a line of thinking. These include the role of public funding for the arts, the role of arts institutions, the relevance of the activities undertaken in relation to the wider population, access to knowledge of what is being undertaken, and access to the activities themselves, whether financial, physical or 'emotional'.

It should be borne in mind that at the beginning of the project, only seven entries under the LS9 7 postal code (for Ebor Gardens) appeared in the WYP marketing database, which totals 140,000 entries,[2] and of a 'Heydays'[3] membership of 700, none were from the Ebor Gardens Estate. The WYP aspiration to be 'a club of which everyone can consider themselves to be a member'[4] did not appear to resonate at this early stage of the programme, certainly so far as the nearest community residents were concerned.

For the WYP this project was therefore a high-risk venture from the outset. It might reveal that the theatre is irrelevant to whole sections of the population, including its closest neighbours: its very public aspirations for developing cultural democracy could be blown out of the water. It might even be accused of attempting a kind of 'cultural colonisation' that might well be frowned upon if attempted with countries on the other side of the world.

What was not sufficiently expressed in the initial proposal to the Joseph Rowntree Foundation was the extent to which the Playhouse could be a beneficiary of the project. As the year unfolded it was to become clear that the Playhouse had much more to gain than ticket sales and political credibility, and that this was to be a significant learning experience for the entire organisation.

On the basis of WYP's application, a research project over a period of one year was agreed, whereby JRF would finance both a limited intervention by the WYP in the local community and an external evaluation of the process. In line with usual JRF practice, an Advisory Group was drawn together to support the project. The group harnessed expertise from local residents, the arts funding system, research and central government.

In response to a strong steer from the Advisory Group, the Playhouse set out its own initial aims and objectives, of necessity without reference to the local community. It was important to capture the expectations of the Playhouse in entering into this partnership. This gave the Playhouse a benchmark against which to review what subsequently happened. It was always the expectation that the initial aims and objectives would need to be reframed.

Aim

To generate a productive and sustainable relationship between the community of Ebor Gardens and the West Yorkshire Playhouse.

Objectives

1 Over the course of a year, to increase the range and quality of what the Playhouse offers the community.
2 To increase the take-up by the community of new and existing WYP services and products, through improved accessibility.
3 To increase the awareness and commitment of the whole WYP institution and its staff to supporting the needs and aspirations of the local community.

Methods

1 To review existing contacts, and make new contacts with local community leaders and service providers.
2 To review past and existing activities offered by WYP, and their local take-up to date.
3 To propose new activities to progress the above aims and objectives.
4 To establish a group of local consultants to participate in this work and to propose, with WYP staff, activities for the remainder of the project.
5 To bring in additional inputs by relevant artists and organisations to deliver the above aims and objectives.

Measurable outcomes

1 An increase in the number of local residents involved in WYP activities.
2 An increase in the range of activities on offer.
3 An increase in the knowledge of, and the deliberate attempts to support, the needs and aspirations of the local community, by WYP staff as a whole.
4 An increase in the local community's awareness of, and satisfaction with, the products and services offered by WYP.

The Playhouse did not propose any target numbers for the above outcomes. Given the nature of inner city estates, it would be almost impossible to obtain definitive statistical data on changes in activity, and in any case it would be unwise to ascribe any particular changes to the intervention by the Playhouse through 'In our neighbourhood'. Instead, effort went into describing changes in attitude and activity, backed wherever possible with available numerical evidence.

It should be stressed that with a project lasting one year only, an enduring impact cannot be reliably recorded or predicted. The involvement of a small number of individuals may only show a real impact after a considerable period of time (and even then not necessarily on the local community, given the past tendency for population transience in the area).

chapter 2

Background

The theatre

Throughout England there exists a network of regional repertory theatre companies, each receiving significant public subsidy, and each strategically placed, in its own purpose-built premises, to serve the artistic needs of communities outside London. Their 'bill of fare' varies to some extent to reflect local interests and demographic variations, but coincides considerably, each one delivering a balance of 'classics' (often feeding schools' National Curriculum demands), popular contemporary plays by the likes of Ayckbourn and Godber, and a certain amount of new writing. There may well be seasonal variations, such as a family-oriented production around the Christmas period, and productions for children during the summer period, and the overall shape of the production schedule would provide no major surprises for anyone moving from one theatre to the next. The general perception is of a fairly stable service being provided for a well-educated, economically secure, socially confident and ageing clientele.

Reflecting the objectives of the Arts Council for England, as enshrined in its Charter, each theatre fulfils an education remit, although the extent of their educational activities varies in accordance with their interpretation of what constitutes an education policy. A few companies still maintain a Theatre in Education Company, though far fewer than in the 1970s and 80s. Their work has focused largely on providing a service for schools, in schools, usually linked to National Curriculum or to 'whole-school' curriculum needs.

Some theatres have interpreted their educational responsibilities much more widely, developing links with higher and further education, creating 'life-long learning' opportunities, and exploring educational aspects of what is broadly described as 'community development'. This latter area encompasses social interaction, health improvement, environmental regeneration, crime reduction and the care of the most needy or vulnerable members of communities – amongst others. Theatres are constantly attempting to define how their primary functions and areas of expertise – the deployment of a wealth of skills and techniques needed for the successful mounting of theatrical productions – can best be made available to the communities they serve.

The use of the word 'communities' here is significant. There has been a growing recognition and sophistication in understanding that theatres do not best relate to 'the community' as a homogeneous mass, but rather that they must consider the varying needs of distinct communities, be they defined by geography, interest or background. They have to balance this sense of differences of needs, interests and tastes with the practicalities of providing a programme of performances and activities which will appeal to as large a range of potential 'buyers' as possible. They also have the responsibility, as artists, to present what they believe in, and what they judge to be of the highest possible artistic value. Within considerable social, financial and political constraints, they need a clear and confident vision to remain successful – and sane.

Leeds Playhouse was established in 1970, one of a wave of new regional theatres created around that time. It was located on the townward side of the campus of Leeds University in a strikingly unremarkable box of a building, shaded by the chimney of the Leeds General Infirmary power station, and abutted by the University sports centre. Its physical profile in the town was not high!

Inside the breeze-block box was placed a remarkably effective auditorium – a hybrid between a proscenium and an arena playing area. (This spatial arrangement, with its capacity to place theatre with the audience, rather than in front of it, was copied with the building of the new theatre, and perhaps gives a clue to the attitude of the theatre board to the relationship between theatre and the communities it serves.) This accounted for a very major part of the cubic capacity of the box. Although the public areas were of a human scale compared with some theatre buildings, they provided little scope for activities other than queuing for seats, tickets or drinks. Administrative and backstage facilities were so limited that Portakabins in the car park were necessary for survival.

Given these circumstances, it is remarkable that the theatre enjoyed two decades of considerable success, attracting and maintaining a very loyal following. However, there was little opportunity for the development of the potential services that are now taken for granted in the West Yorkshire

Playhouse. Even the Leeds Theatre in Education Company, one of the longest established and most respected such companies in the country, had to be housed off-site, first in the disused Gaumont Cinema and then in a local primary school. Not surprisingly, this wing of the operation had a rather distant relationship with the theatre itself.

Although the theatre's local clientele were loyal, and refreshed on a regular basis by the ever-replenishing student population, the relationship with the city of Leeds as a whole was under-exploited. (It is then perhaps curious that the word 'Leeds' should be dropped from the title of the institution at the very moment that it became so much more central to the life of Leeds as a whole. However, this change was in recognition of the substantial contribution given by the then-West Yorkshire County Council toward the building of the new theatre.)

In 1990, the West Yorkshire Playhouse was established on the site of the old Quarry Hill Flats, close to the famous Leeds City Markets, the Central Police Station and the relocated headquarters of the National Health Service. It was the last purpose-built theatre of its kind in the twentieth century.

While the move to new premises posed a perceived threat of distancing the theatre from one of its main markets (the University population), it also created the opportunity to become a much more central part of the life of the town itself. The full spectrum of the population would inevitably become much more aware of it. It became a landmark building, being so visible from a network of major roads, surrounded by busy commercial and administrative centres, and accessible for people arriving by public and private transport. The move not only put the Playhouse in the centre of Leeds life, but also made it a prominent facility for the rest of West Yorkshire and beyond.

The West Yorkshire Playhouse

The arrival did not go unnoticed by new neighbours from the estate:

> **"It was good compared to what was on that site before."**

> **"It's better having it at Quarry Hill than at the university – now the ordinary people can go there too."**

The new building itself created a host of new opportunities. The public spaces (foyer, bar and restaurant) are spacious and airy, allowing for exhibitions, performances, informal meetings and simply relaxation. Meeting rooms, rehearsal spaces, workshop facilities and administration offices are all under one roof (although the price of success is that the building was full to bursting within the first couple of years!).

The relocation and redesigning of the physical concept of repertory theatre coincided with the recruitment of a different style of management. Jude Kelly, the artistic director, came from a background of young people's theatre (Solent People's Theatre), a community arts centre (Battersea), and her own community-oriented version of the York Mystery Plays. Given her new facility, she quickly established a structure that would exploit the potential to relate to a much greater cross-section of the population. A whole community and education section was formed, to develop artistic and creative opportunities both within and outside the premises. For instance, the schools touring operation was brought into the building and various techniques were used to ensure that the theatre would become well known as a facility for the public within and beyond Leeds.

The very high – and very positive – profile of the theatre attracted demands, expectations and responsibilities. Over the years it has become part of the public face of Leeds, and has been successfully exploited as such. In particular, the Playhouse has featured very prominently in publications and brochures aimed at attracting inward investment to the city. In a city that has experienced enormous growth, especially in the financial services sector, the Playhouse has been marketed as a significant attraction to professionals considering relocation to Leeds.

The Playhouse has also established a strong record as a corporate entertainment experience, using its function rooms and catering facilities as part of a complete package of play-going for commercial organisations throughout the region. This responsibility to contribute to the development of Leeds as a whole combines well with the need to maximise income from the facilities, but inevitably puts pressure on the various departments to deliver the goods. Community development, of the type envisaged in the 'In our neighbourhood' project, in some ways competes with the range of priorities facing the organisation.

However, during the last three years it could be argued that the local 'business' orientation has been counterbalanced by the national focus on education and community development, and on issues such as social inclusion and lifelong learning. As is the case with so many cultural institutions, the Playhouse could rightly claim that it was always concerned with those issues, but one might well assume that a central government promotion of such concerns could only result in even greater attention to such matters.

People come from far and wide to use the Playhouse building. It is a hub for those who want to learn about innovative ideas.

The community

One side of the WYP site is bordered by the A64, one of the busiest arterial roads into the city of Leeds, and part of a rapid access route through the city centre. Where it passes the Playhouse, it is a striking example of a communication route doubling as a physical barrier. The road is raised up on a flyover, with a web of access roads laid beneath it. Negotiating the area by car at certain times of day is not for the faint hearted, and apart for a vertigo-inducing footbridge over the entire system, pedestrian access from the North to the South side of the A64 can be bewildering and disturbing.

This physical hurdle divides the West Yorkshire Playhouse from its nearest residential community, the Ebor Gardens Estate. While access to the new theatre for the populations of Leeds and West Yorkshire in general has been vastly improved by the relocation to its present site, the level of improvement for the new neighbours has been disproportionately low. For many young people, less fazed by the terrors of modern traffic, the WYP is directly on their everyday route between home, school and the centre of town, which for many is less than ten minutes' walk from home. For older people, and parents encumbered by fast and active children and baby buggies, the Playhouse is particularly difficult to reach.

In order to give an impression of the estate, some features are noted:

- The estate comprises approximately 1,140 dwellings with a population of approximately 3,000.
- Three years ago, the annual population turnover was around 41 per cent, but this is now at around 23 per cent per annum.
- Housing tenure is very mixed, and includes a number of housing associations, owner-occupiers and council-owned and managed properties.
- There is a broad mix of ethnic origins, family configurations and age groups.

The Playhouse lies directly behind the building housing the national headquarters of the DSS (visible in the background), which overlooks a section of the estate. This picture also shows traffic calming measures implemented during refurbishment.

- Although many pupils move over the 'boundaries' of the estate for schooling, most attend Ebor Gardens Primary School, and Agnes Stewart High School, although the latter is actually over a main road bordering the estate.

A number of issues of particular concern have been identified by various interviewees in the course of this research:

- the transitory nature of the population
- the high crime rate
- the incidence of drug dependency, and consequent exposure of young people to that danger
- the number of children in care (the highest percentage in the city)
- poverty, as evidenced by a 61 per cent take-up of free school meals
- low self-esteem among both individuals and the community
- lack of community identity
- isolation of the elderly population, aggravated by transport difficulties.

Several interviewees have identified a high level of tolerance among the population, especially concerning racial origins, single parent families, and lifestyle choices. Children grow up in an environment of terrific social diversity, perhaps more so than in most other areas of the city:[5]

> "Ethnic mix on the estate is seen to be a strength. It leads to a tolerance that may be absent elsewhere – and at least a familiarity with other cultures. It applies also to understanding and acceptance of gay relationships within families, of which there are many on the estate. It does not have the stigma attached that might be more so in middle-class areas. Awareness of unusualness and family differences leads to more positive attitudes."
>
> *Local teacher*

If the WYP experienced a rebirth in 1990, so during the subsequent ten years did its neighbour, Ebor Gardens Estate. Seeking guidance on the development needs of the estate, Leeds City Council commissioned a report from housing consultants Chapman Hendy, which was submitted in 1991. Their report not only audited and made recommendations concerning the physical condition of the estate, it also assessed the social fabric of the estate, acknowledging that 'physical refurbishment of the housing will not, on its own, stem the decline in Ebor Gardens' fortunes'.

The report identifies a range of issues where statistical and perceptual data indicate a striking level of dereliction, while pointing out that these are common in estates that are in decline in any other part of the country. While stressing that this picture is now ten years out of date, and not wishing to stereotype the image of Ebor Gardens, it is worth looking back on the state of affairs at the beginning of the 1990s:

> 'The Ebor Gardens estate is tangibly in decline. Other estates have perhaps more visible signs of decay and dereliction, of vandalism and neglect than has Ebor Gardens, but the deterioration in the social fabric of the estate is all too apparent, and is accelerating.
>
> 'The downward spiral which Ebor Gardens is now experiencing is recognised by outsiders from other parts of Leeds: "It's not a good area…it's a dumping ground".
>
> 'It is felt keenly by professional workers on, and responsible for, the estate, by public

authorities, and most forcibly of all by the residents themselves. In the household survey covered by section A2, 80 per cent of respondents felt that the general condition of the estate was deteriorating; one-third of respondents were actively seeking a transfer out of the area.

'Physical refurbishment of the housing will not, on its own, stem the decline in Ebor Garden's fortunes; *[the Chapman Hendy report highlights]* some of the social issues and describe some of the factors it will be necessary to understand and to tackle, in order to plan a successful regeneration of Ebor Gardens.

'Although it has many locational advantages – proximity to the centre of the city, adequate transport links, shops and healthcare facilities relatively near at hand – the triangle which is Ebor Gardens estate is isolated and cut off by the major roads which border it. This creates a psychological if not a physical barrier to many of the residents there, many of whom cannot, or will not through fear, lack of money, lack of confidence, venture out of their estate. In these circumstances the quality of local facilities becomes very important.

'Ebor Gardens is unequivocally an estate "on the margins". Already a very serious mix of economic and social problems are being manifested. Concerns have been expressed about the levels of poverty, indebtedness, money-lending, child abuse, use of drugs, solvent abuse and crimes against property on the estate. Unemployment is high, expectations are low. The threshold of normality within the estate is progressively being lowered.'[6]

Physical proximity might not mean physical accessibility, of course. And there are other barriers can also segregate a community from the services that it might enjoy. Economics, self-image, prejudice (in either direction), lack of information and an inappropriate match of needs and provision could all contribute to a lack of relationship between, in this example, a theatre and its neighbouring community.

The project reviewed in this report aimed to explore and develop such a relationship. It identified some of the barriers, and some of the techniques that can enable a community to make use of social facilities. But perhaps its greatest strength was in developing a relationship with the community and with individuals, and finding out how the parties to a relationship were able to explore each other's needs and potential for their mutual benefit.

The 'In our neighbourhood' project revealed that the people of Ebor Gardens didn't really feel excluded from the Playhouse – they just didn't see it as relevant to their lives, and though it was there, they saw no need to engage with it. There were a few negative attitudes at the time of the Playhouse's relocation:

> **"I think people always thought of the Playhouse as very off limits, snobby, overpriced place. They used to walk past saying 'That's not for me, you'd have to dress up.' And 'I thought it was a waste of money 10 years ago – I've changed my mind now.'"**
> **Resident**

But for most people interviewed in this research, the Playhouse was neither here nor there. In the words of one community worker, "It might as well be a million miles away."

chapter 3

The 1990s and the context of development

Both parties to the 'In our neighbourhood' project were affected by extraordinary change over the past ten years resulting in physical transformation and new opportunities. They have certainly shared with other institutions and communities the plethora of developmental initiatives emanating from central, local and quasi-governmental sources. They have also been subjected to the various trends in management and organisational thinking which have pervaded public and commercial life during the last quarter of the twentieth century.

Primary amongst these is the accelerating rate of change itself. Although this has not been caused by deliberate government policy, it has radically influenced the ways in which policy has been framed over recent years. Among the most obvious responses to the accelerating speed of change is the tendency for administrations to favour short-term projects and funding. Where historically inert funding patterns had previously existed, often favouring moribund organisations, projects now often lack the time in which to mature and learn from their experiences. This in turn fed a consumer habit of transience, never expecting anything to last, be it material products or community activities. Community habits and traditions have no time to establish before funding runs out or a new initiative is thrust upon the population.

Consequently, local organisers find it hard to juggle the demands of an ever-growing portfolio of projects, or indeed to supply the individuals from the community to take part in those initiatives. Such 'initiative fatigue' is often described in the context of formal education, but equally applies in community contexts.

Of Ebor Gardens, one voluntary community worker stated, "On this estate they've gone from having nothing to having a hell of a lot." The statement was a very positive response to the developments that have taken place on the estate over the last ten years. But there is a downside. There is a perceived pressure to deliver projects that are initiated from above, if only to make use of the funding attached to those projects. However, this does not necessarily coincide with the needs on the ground, or the pace at which change can be healthily absorbed.

Related to this short-termism is the requirement for instant, measurable outputs. If a project is to be funded only for one, two or three years, there is a demand to prove the validity of the investment within that time. This may overlook the fact that some developments take at least that time to gestate, and often longer to show any evidence of benefit. In such cases, the pressure to demonstrate statistical successes over a short time may obscure an understanding of longer term effectiveness and value.

Examples of short, or at least fixed term projects that require very clearly defined and quantifiable outputs are Single Regeneration Budgets, European Social Fund projects and National Lottery Grants. The impact of these three alone on both West Yorkshire Playhouse and Ebor Gardens is very considerable. Managing the activities arising from these funding sources in order to achieve long-lasting beneficial effects is a great challenge for those working at the delivery end. Being statistically accountable is not sufficient for those dedicated to improving the quality of life rather than the quantity of output.

Also linked to the rate of change in society generally is the tendency for activity to fragment. At the personal level, individuals tend to stay within their own homes more, relating less and less to those around them, for whatever reasons. As consumers, we expect to be served as individuals, making individual choices concerning products and services, and to a considerable extent this is deliverable, at least within the field of consumer products. However, this ethos puts tremendous pressure on public services, often operating on slimmed down resources and staffing. Pressure of work within organisations can result in less communication with other agencies or departments, and so fragmentation forms a vicious circle.

Two reactive responses can emerge from administrations. The first is to attempt to streamline and co-ordinate services, encouraging 'joined-up' administration. However, in the short term this can be perceived as another contributor to 'initiative fatigue' which itself can result in strained or even resentful co-ordination. While the impetus is laudable, the need to obtain instant results can ignore the human pace at which interactive changes need to take place.

The second response is to 'batch' developmental activities, imposing upon them consistent rules concerning aims, planning, application procedures and monitoring. In order to cope with variations between projects, these procedures can become long and convoluted, and consequently very exacting for those delivering on the ground. Ebor Gardens residents and community workers have expressed concern that project establishment can be too bureaucratic, and not at the pace needed by the potential participants.

One of the most prevalent trends in the delivery of public services is the encouragement of partnership approaches. In the context of community development, partnerships between local government and the voluntary sector are increasingly important. In some cases, the local authority contracts a voluntary agency to deliver certain required services. This is less about partnership than a commissioner/provider relationship. In others, agencies will collaborate to provide activities that are seen to deliver their own overlapping agendas.

The relationship between the Playhouse and Ebor Gardens could be seen to be such a partnership. The local authority, through its community centre and its staff, provides premises, expertise and access to the community, while the Playhouse delivers its own expertise, services and access to the theatre. The Playhouse agenda is to fulfil its responsibility to reach a wider cross-section of the community, and in so doing increase the use of its services. The local authority creates access to facilities and expertise that it believes will enhance the quality of life on the estate, with the effect of reducing some of the social difficulties facing such a community.

The partnership cannot operate as a service provider/consumer relationship, in that the service to be provided, and the needs to be addressed, are not static or defined. What each partner brings to the relationship may be very apparent and to some extent definable, but the outcome of their collaboration can only be discovered through experience.

For individuals on both sides there is no precedent. While a few of the Playhouse staff have experienced successful projects in other communities, they have not been on this scale, or over twelve months, and the theatre itself has had only limited dealings with residents of inner city council estates. The overwhelming majority of the residents of Ebor Gardens have had no experience of using the facilities of a regional theatre – indeed nationally that is true of a very large proportion of the entire population. For a variety of reasons, the majority of the residents on the estate have little experience of using any of the cultural facilities in the city other than the cinema or bingo, although a small number do attend some of the excellent concerts at the Leeds Irish Centre.

So the 'In our neighbourhood' project poses two questions:

- What can a regional theatre contribute to the social fabric of a rapidly improving inner city housing estate?
- What can an inner city housing estate contribute to the development of a vibrant regional theatre?

This project, like so many others in the current context, is a short-term intervention. To fulfil its objectives requires a statistical increase in usage of the Playhouse or its services. It is yet another initiative to be accommodated by the community workers on the estate. Seeing beyond the initial outputs to the longer term outcomes is itself fraught with difficulties. However, in this case, the funding arrangements and the commitment of the parties to the relationship means that the focus is on the quality of the experience generated during the course of the project. Given the low level of involvement between the residents of Ebor Gardens and the West Yorkshire Playhouse at the start of the project, no one expected mass attendance at performances or other activities. Instead, what has been sought is significant involvement that can lead to a discernible transformation in the lives of individuals, and in the effectiveness of the community as a whole.

chapter 4

Ten years of change

Between 1990 and 1999, before the start of the 'In our neighbourhood' project, both parties to the relationship have made strides forward in terms of activity and aspirations. It is very important to acknowledge these before considering the last year's work in any detail. Without the previous decade of development, the last year of development would not have been possible, and any outcomes, for the community and residents of Ebor Gardens, and for the Playhouse itself, may well be as much the product of ten years of change as of twelve months of activity.

Developments at the West Yorkshire Playhouse

The relocation and re-invention of the theatre in Leeds has already been described above. Here we look at some of the initiatives undertaken at WYP aimed at making the institution more relevant and accessible to a wider population.

The design of the Playhouse building was significantly informed by a desire to be open to the community. Its location and exterior architectural style were intended to be as welcoming as possible to passers-by. The interior spaces were conceived with human scale in mind, so as not to be in any way forbidding to those unused to visiting cultural establishments. However, early attitudes to the Playhouse were not always positive:

"Why do we need another one? We'd got the Playhouse at the University, the Grand, City Varieties – why do we need another one? I went past it when I used to go to town, but I never went in, not until there was a visit from my daughter's school and they needed more adults with them. That would have been about four years ago. When I went in I said, 'Have they finished it?' because the walls and the design are so different from ordinary old-type theatres. There were no curtains."

This attitude, expressed by a mother on the estate prior to the 'In our neighbourhood' project, was not entirely representative. The quote was from a resident who had actually crossed the threshold within the first five years of the theatre's arrival. Most residents, although passing the front door on a regular basis while travelling to and from town, wouldn't even think of entering:

"I've never even been in to have a look. I've gone past it many a time to go to the market."

"You're never sure what it's going to be like, are you?"

There is no doubt that the theatre is regarded as entirely accessible by vast numbers of people. The restaurant and bar area is used by hundreds of people each week: many people regularly use the

The Playhouse's attempts to involve the community in the day-to-day activities of the WYP included encouraging the use of existing facilities such as its cybercafé.

bar and restaurant for social and business meetings (quite apart from those using it before, during and after performances). The meeting rooms are booked almost to saturation, and there is a very full schedule of activities in them, in the rehearsal rooms and in the foyer spaces. One of the most noticeable of these is the weekly Heydays sessions, providing a range of cultural and creative activities for the over-55s. However, just because the facility is fully subscribed, one should not assume that it is universally accessible.

> "No we haven't been to Heydays. It's very clannish – very snobbish – and that's from someone who still goes there. If you go on your own, you're on your own. You're not made welcome…There's this woman who goes and she was saying she likes it, that it's a different class of people there."
>
> *Local resident*

These attitudes are clearly not shared by those many regulars who do attend Heydays, and the perception may not match the reality for those members. However, perceptions are as real as experience, and can create hurdles in reaching those sections of the community who regard themselves, rightly or wrongly, as being excluded.

As well as its physical facilities, the Playhouse has been at pains to make its expertise available to the community. Staff across all departments make themselves available to give talks and demonstrations for groups at all levels of education. For example, the Playhouse Partners scheme negotiates learning programmes with individual schools, adult education classes on various aspects of theatre are run in conjunction with the universities, tours of the theatre are organised for all sorts of groups, and one-to-one advice is often provided for individuals seeking specialist expertise. Most of these activities take place in the building, exploiting the physical as well as the staffing potential, but a range of services are also offered off-site in education and community premises.

A less direct service to the community is also provided by exploiting the profile of the theatre. The Director, Jude Kelly, uses her own position to advocate nationally the role of the arts and creativity in the social and community development of the population. The premises are frequently used as a platform for events and conferences concerning the role of the arts, and many of these are organised by the Playhouse itself. Amongst these have been events concerning pre-school education, the arts and offenders, and launch events for national arts and education initiatives. Many of these have led to ongoing activities for particular groups, such as creative play sessions for parents and toddlers.

Finally, the Playhouse has made strenuous attempts to make access more widely available to its primary product, the plays presented on the stages. Again, although attendances have been consistently good since the Playhouse opened, not everyone feels that they can make use of the facilities.

> **"I didn't go at first, because without enquiring about it, I thought it would be too dear for me. That was the first thing. You associate theatre with things going on in London and those prices you know."**
>
> *Local resident*

Enquiries over the past ten years about reduced ticket prices would have elicited different responses at different times. There have been experiments with free tickets for unemployed people on certain nights, group rates have been very competitive, and concessions for various sectors have consistently been made available. Of most relevance to this particular study is the Community Network scheme, launched in 1996. This allows registered community groups to make group bookings at extremely reduced prices, and much more will be said about this scheme later in the report.

Refurbished housing, improved streetlighting and traffic calming contribute to a sense of security.

Overall, the West Yorkshire Playhouse has explored an impressive range of strategies to encourage the widest possible usage of the facilities and services available. Not only have the activities been carefully developed with this in mind, but the attitudes of the staff have been a crucial element in making the broadest cross-section of the population feel welcome.

The often referred to absence of a 'stage door' is one manifestation of the attempts to break down the barrier between arts professionals and the public, and it is abundantly clear that all kinds of people are welcome in the theatre. However, despite all of these efforts, the reality is that the uptake of the inhabitants of the nearest residential area, Ebor Gardens, had not been significant. 'In our neighbourhood' sought to explore and address this fact.

A 'Learning Partnership' initiative involved residents in the refurbishment of the estate – here, replanting the gardens outside the community centre.

Developments at Ebor Gardens

As described earlier in this report, Ebor Gardens has had its problems. The Chapman Hendy report described this in compelling terms. However, that report proposed a catalogue of improvements that have transformed life on the estate for a large number of people.

The physical refurbishment of the estate has been widely praised by the interviewees. For many, aspects of security had been deep concerns prior to refurbishment. Residents had been afraid to leave their homes unattended for fear of burglary or vandalism. New windows and locks might seem like fairly basic improvements, but the effect for many, especially older residents, has been dramatic.

The introduction of closed circuit television (CCTV) cameras has been a further contribution to the sense of security. Having left their homes, many residents were also fearful of moving around the estate, especially across open spaces or poorly lit and concealed pathways. But once CCTV had been installed, confidence increased:

"Currently there's a very low crime rate on the estate, moving it from the fifteenth worst estate in Leeds for crime to the second-best. It's mainly brought about by environmental and security improvements,

A refurbished child-friendly play facility.

and also better tenant recruitment by Leeds City Council. As a result, people are willing to leave their flats and houses unattended for the first time in seven years. Tenants' associations are becoming very active – the success of the estate is becoming the envy of neighbouring estates, who now want to join up with Ebor in community forums, etc., so the Torries area is joining in now."

Community worker

Traffic calming devices, and an enhanced sense of well-being generated by the improved environment, have also promoted a willingness to be out and about. For some older residents, this harks back to happier days when a stronger sense of community existed in the area:

"I missed the row of trees when they refurbished the estate, but I've moved now, so that's alright. It's just that you get different people coming to the estate, and they keep themselves to themselves. We used to sit outside on our chairs, shouting to each other, you know, but we don't now. It is starting up again now where I used to live – there's a couple up there who do – I think it's this couple – they really like the outdoors."

Local resident

The festive period around Christmas and the New Year provided further evidence of a growing confidence on the estate:

"This estate has a real community spirit. All the tenants' associations are growing. We don't need to talk all the time now about physical improvements – that's largely done. Now it's about social development. People are talking in the street, even going for a walk around which they wouldn't have done before. Neighbours are talking to each other. It was a very positive Christmas period for mutual support. A lot of it is because people are feeling safe about leaving their homes unattended. Last Christmas we had 30 burglaries over the Christmas period – this year none. And the centre is becoming much more active."

Community worker

This very upbeat appraisal of the situation is of course informed by the timing of the interview, immediately after an exceptional millennium celebration, and such subjective comments can vary with changing events, or the frame of mind of the interviewee. Nevertheless, such comments would have been most unlikely in the not too distant past.

Provision for older residents was good – the luncheon club and bingo, both held at the community centre, were particularly popular.

The reference to the increased use of the community centre is significant and a willingness to venture out is only part of the picture. The centre had experienced difficult times prior to the refurbishment process, of which it was a part: the Chapman Hendy report tells a sorry tale of neglect, disrepair, delay and disappointment. Even after the refurbishment, there had been veiled references to the centre being dominated by a very small clique, apparently to the exclusion of others. This problem has been overcome during the last year or so. The pivotal position of the centre in the regeneration of social activities should not be underestimated.

The Chapman Hendy report stressed the need to address social regeneration as well as physical refurbishment if the estate was to become successful. There has been a rapid growth of activities available to residents over the last few years, some generated by the community centre staff, some by voluntary agencies working in the centre, and some with no connection to the centre.

Of the centre-generated activities, among the best used and most enduring are the creche, the weekly art and craft sessions, the luncheon club for senior citizens, a weekly cookery club and a newly formed community café operating two days per week, with support from Education 2000, whose 'Changing communities' project also led to the establishment of the internet project, set up by local volunteers with financial support from local businesses.

Education 2000 (a locally based education charity), now called Learning Partnerships, have been an enduring presence in the area, their intention being to develop learning communities through whatever means are appropriate on the ground. Another voluntary agency with an established relationship to the community is Skippko Arts, who have been working at the community centre, especially with women's groups, since 1995. Park Lane College, a local further education establishment, has also provided valuable education and training opportunities in the area.

Another rapid and dramatic development has been the increased number of tenants' and residents' associations on the estate. These have both practical and social remits, and have become very significant in the relationship with the Playhouse, of which more later. A community forum, established as an essential means of communication during the refurbishment process, remains intact, but may well be replaced by another body once the planned Community Involvement Team is established on the estate. (At the time of writing, this had been delayed beyond the projected start date, and behind the establishment of similar teams in other parts of the city.)

It is in the context of such rapid and fundamental changes that the WYP project, 'In our neighbourhood', takes place. But as will be seen in the following pages, the theatre's experience of working with the Ebor Gardens residents was that work involving communities needs to happen at a pace appropriate to the community – ideas often need time to settle and be embraced. Sometimes things can happen at an exciting pace. Most of all, it is necessary to keep a clear focus on objectives in order to avoid being railroaded by events while retaining the ability to respond to developing needs and perceptions.

Part II

The process

chapter 5

Stage one: First contacts

For the last two years the manager of Ebor Gardens' community centre has, along with enthusiastic residents, been building up an identity for the centre, while having to operate around a succession of builders and decorators. Prior to her arrival, the centre had a 'difficult' history. It had been underused, and there were obscure references to it being dominated by a local family; a combination of this history, a transient population, and a culture of non-involvement and social 'apartheid' all presented a formidable obstacle to progress.

So, given that the local population had not been inclined to use even their own centre, it was hardly surprising that the West Yorkshire Playhouse should seem like such an alien structure. A community worker described the Playhouse thus:

> "A lot of people walk past its front door at least once a week on their way into town, but for most people around here, it might as well be a million miles away."

By contrast, October 1999 at the West Yorkshire Playhouse couldn't have looked more different. It seemed almost over-used, with the massive and diverse cast for *Carnival Messiah* bringing in the widest cross-section of the Leeds population that it had ever attracted. Add to that the more traditional audiences for *Macbeth*, the 'arty' clientele for *DV8* and the stalwarts for the Heydays sessions, and one might be forgiven for thinking that this was the cultural centre for the entire population of Leeds. Yet on its very doorstep was a whole community making virtually no connection with the Playhouse at all.

Given the need to establish a fuller use of Ebor Gardens' community centre, it may at first sight seem surprising that local workers should embrace an initiative by the West Yorkshire Playhouse aimed at developing a relationship between the community and WYP, even going so far as to host an event aimed at introducing the Playhouse to the local population.

But community interests are wider than the walls of the community centre, and if the WYP workers could encourage opportunities for the estate residents, and use the centre resources to do so, then that's what would be done. If that meant greater use of the centre, then so much the better. So began the 'In our neighbourhood' project.

First moves

Although the WYP had made the approach to the Joseph Rowntree Foundation as sole applicant, it already had some sporadic and uncoordinated engagement with the local community. It also had experience of working with communities from other parts of the city not used to using the theatre, and of arranging arts activities well beyond the normal or mainstream activities of a producing repertory theatre. This, together with the reputation and status of the WYP, served to open doors when making contacts with key players in the community. A series of meetings was arranged with 'gatekeepers' to the community, including local social services managers, a local volunteer co-ordinator and a redevelopment supervisor, which served the process well in terms of making new contacts and identifying local needs and preoccupations.

Various questions arose. What geographical area will be covered? What are the key issues facing the community? Who would be the most appropriate people to target in the earliest stages of the project? What timescale would be the most effective? What exactly could the WYP best contribute, or draw attention to, as a means of opening dialogue with the community? What's in it for the community?

A small but significant network of community workers and volunteers was quickly identified. A very few of these were already known to the WYP, and more were contacted each week. The team of workers at the WYP envisaged using a technique that they had successfully employed on another project to research and introduce the programme for the coming year. This would involve a small group of local 'consultants' creating some form of presentation, perhaps in performance, video or exhibition form, which might propose how the relationship could develop.

A small and fluid core of these workers and volunteers met on a number of consecutive Thursdays to undertake this task, working closely with a team of five WYP staff. A local artist set up a small exhibition of pictures about the changing nature of the estate as an example

of what might be produced, and a number of disposable cameras were issued to residents to take photos of what they felt was good and bad about the estate. But the real work of the local consultants, with the WYP staff, was the planning of a day event in the community centre to 'launch' the idea of a relationship with the WYP.

The opening event

The day would be split into two parts: lunchtime and early afternoon would be devoted to activities aimed at members of the luncheon club, which usually comprised around 20 elderly residents assembling for a lunch provided by 'Meals on Wheels'. After a short break, the second part of the event would be aimed at parents and children returning home from school.

The Playhouse wardrobe hire department agreed to bring along a selection of costumes for attenders to try on and be photographed in. Playhouse catering agreed to provide light refreshments. The WYP team also engaged the services of a circus skills expert, a face painter, and a Mendhi (henna hand tattooing) specialist; and the local artist organised craft materials and activities. Although initially agreeing to appear, a local rock band eventually withdrew their services.

As so often happens, not everything went according to plan. The 'Meals on Wheels' service had a staffing crisis and so there was no luncheon. Consequently, the transport to bring in the elderly had to be cancelled. And it rained. The result was that there were no elderly people present on the day. However, a few adults with young children popped in to see what was going on. Protesting that they would have to be off any minute, they stayed all afternoon, leaving only for long enough to collect other children from school and bring them back too.

By 3.30pm there were approximately fifty people attending and this figure remained roughly constant until closing time at around 5.30p.m. In all, a total of perhaps 70 people attended. Of these, roughly 40 per cent were under the age of 11, 40 per cent were adults, and 20 per cent were adolescents. Of the adolescents, several were part of the photography group from Agnes Stewart High School, brought along by their teacher to record the event. According to centre staff, many were faces not seen before in the centre.

The event was very active. The costume department did a roaring trade all afternoon, as did both hand painting and face painting. Although often diffident at first, many children tried out various circus skills, and, apparently uncharacteristically, were self-disciplined in sharing the use of the available equipment.

A steady flow of people, adults and children, made Halloween masks and cards with the craft materials, food was consumed at a steady rate, and names, comments and ticks appeared on the various sheets seeking information about future interest. Adults appeared to be relaxed and engaged throughout the time, withdrawing occasionally for a quiet chat outside in the drizzle, and then returning to the festivities.

Post-event soundings

Twelve days after the event, two of the WYP team and two of the local consultants met to review the day and consider the future in the light of it. In spite of the disappointment over the luncheon club

misfortune, the reaction from the centre's workers was extremely positive:

"A lot of people came in who wouldn't usually come in. A number of people said what a lovely atmosphere it was. One woman said it was the first time she'd felt almost a community spirit here."

The centre manager felt strongly that the style and tenor of the event worked particularly well:

"It confirmed what I already thought. That it needs to be laid back and unpressurised. They won't be pushed."

There was surprise and satisfaction that so many people had attended the event, especially given the unfortunate luncheon club failure and the inclement weather. The publicity for the event was held to be largely responsible for this. There was also clear delight that people had been so involved in the activities on offer, and not only the children.

Attendees had filled in sheets inviting comments and ideas for the future and, more importantly, ideas had been expressed in conversation:

"Some were saying on the day, 'Could we go and have a look round *[the Playhouse]*?' – maybe half a dozen people asked that, all quite unprompted. They were saying things like, 'Oh, they're quite nice,' and 'We didn't know they did this kind of thing,' instead of the usual 'It's not for me.' Now people are talking about the possibility of setting up a drama group. About four people in the residents' association have mentioned that."
Resident

Other ideas for future activities were met with considerable interest by people at the event. These included dance sessions, a Christmas party, and more events of this nature. The meeting itself generated a considerable list of possible future activities, which included youth and community worker training sessions in the arts, a variety of ways of using the Playhouse itself more fully, more sustained arts projects at the centre, and further social events, initially occurring around Christmas.

The impact on the community

Beyond the instant satisfaction generated by the event itself, it would have been foolish to attempt to identify any wider impact at that stage. The timeliness of the event, coinciding with the near-completion of the estate refurbishment, might indicate a potential for the WYP intervention to be very productive. Even at this early stage certain potential outcomes were becoming apparent which the project was able to usefully bear in mind in strategically planning future moves.

For example, the 'sense of community' referred to above was clearly a fundamental aim:

"The need is to make the estate more settled and permanent."

Community worker

One worker referred to a conversation about planning future activities in the community:

"People are beginning to take an interest in themselves. Talking about the future, one woman said, 'I don't see myself as having a future – I just live day to day.' The fact she could say that is in a way an advance; at least she's not just keeping that to herself. We need to do things that enable people to think about their lives."

The fact that the event drew in new attenders in such unexpected numbers, engendered a sense of community, however transient, and revealed an interest in exploring the neighbour's back yard (the WYP), all suggested the stirrings of a confidence which might lead to bolder steps in the future.

chapter 6

Stage two: What next ?

At the initial event, residents were already proposing future activities with the WYP. This in itself was very encouraging. It revealed that an interest in developing a 'relationship', whatever that may mean, was already on their agenda. The simple awareness that the WYP was interested in working with the residents, and that there were so many possibilities available, was in itself a break-through. But many questions hung in the air at this stage.

- To what extent will this become a series of 'goodies' delivered by the WYP to the community?
- To what extent will the Playhouse as a whole satisfy the appetites being expressed at this stage by the residents?
- Will residents start to become involved in the existing activities at the WYP to a greater extent?
- Will the momentum be maintained beyond the novelty of the 'first date'?
- If the community responds to the overture, will the WYP respond to the community?

Strategies needed to be developed from the outset to ensure that the community saw themselves as neither 'beneficiaries' nor 'victims' of the interest of their neighbours. So far, the experience was very positive. The centre manager mused further on the 'laid back' approach:

"I've realised I have to place an idea and then give it time to mature before going for any action. We need to have the idea, think about it, let people get comfortable with it – and then do it...Karaoke goes down well. I hate it, but people know what to expect. People don't come in because they don't know what's expected of them."

If that applied to residents' relationship to their own community centre, it must be multiplied up when referring to the less familiar WYP.

The first 'blind date' did work – the residents were intending to see each other again. In the words of a local community activist:

"Outside groups taking an interest in the estate does give a bit of confidence."

Asked what her vision for the 'relationship' a year from now might be, the centre manager responded:

"In a year, people from here will just feel able to use the Playhouse, and the Playhouse people will feel free to come here. For the Playhouse to become theatre for the people by the people. That it's an opportunity for anyone from here to take up. For the Playhouse to be able to come out and help people to develop their talents. That it will become a partnership."

To summarise the project to date, a considerable amount had been achieved by the WYP team in partnership with a small number of local community activists. A level of awareness and familiarity, and hopefully trust, had been established in a short period of time. Appetites had been whetted.

This so far had been based on a single event rather than a development strategy, and might be characterised as a provider/recipient relationship, rather than a partnership effort. The local community, for that event, could be seen as having been in the 'beneficiary' role, which is very akin to the 'victim' role, in that it does not involve any real level of control or influence. The imparting of information, and the generation of an awareness of possibilities, was an essential first step in moving beyond that initially unequal stage of the 'relationship'.

But the WYP needed to preserve the surprise and risk elements that, perhaps uniquely, arts organisations contribute to society. There needed to be a strategy at the front of the mind whereby the community was empowered to take responsibility not only for their own cultural development, but to influence the development of the WYP itself. The rhetoric of cultural democracy, and the undoubted experience of the WYP in working with a diversity of communities, were a potentially sound base from which to explore this new relationship with the local community. The personal and collective sensitivities required in communicating with a population lacking in the confidence or experience of empowerment, might well challenge the entire modus operandi of the WYP if an enduring relationship was to be created.

The 'getting to know you' meeting in October was in its own terms very successful, in that it broke down barriers, established some trust and dialogue, and made the residents see that the WYP workers came as friends with something worth having. Both the Playhouse and the community centre staff emerged from the event energised and with ambitions for developing the relationship.

A host of ideas sprang up, all aimed at capitalising on the sense of achievement. On the one hand there were residents saying, "When are you going to do this again?" On the other, there was an awareness that it would not be possible, or necessarily desirable, to replicate the success of the October event. The following is a list of activities that were proposed for consideration:

- Drama and creative arts workshops for younger children in schools, pre-school playgroups or the centre creche.
- Reviewing existing creative activities and planning new ones for the older people, to include a history/reminiscence project with older residents.
- A freelance worker to be given a roving brief to make contacts and research needs on the estate.
- Developing 'Play at the Playhouse', an on-going project offering workshops for parents with young children, to suit the needs of parents on this estate.
- Youth workers to bring groups of young people to the Playhouse, possibly for a backstage tour.
- Making links with the health centre for workshops such as aromatherapy.

The residents themselves, in making their requests known, asked for the establishment of a drama group, and for backstage visits to the Playhouse. (By no means all of these activities were pursued during the course of the project.)

At the same time, and with further impetus from the October event, plans were under way to set up a user group to organise activities in the centre for the coming year.

While there was a general belief that residents would now feel freer to make demands on both the centre and the Playhouse, there was a cautionary note: be aware of the potentially low confidence of residents to take up what may seem like obvious and simple opportunities. That, combined with the need to move at the pace of the community, meant that the above proposals achieved widely varying levels of success. A considerable amount of work took place, especially in making contacts, but over the two months following the October event, very few Playhouse-led activities took place. The main participatory event to emerge was in fact the Christmas Fair.

Christmas passed...

The Christmas Fair was initially conceived as a week of celebratory activities, some of which would involve inputs from the Playhouse. Events might include trips, parties, lunches, a karaoke night – the idea being to provide something for everyone. Given work pressures all round, this was eventually reduced to an afternoon event incorporating a number of the above activities, timed to attract both older and younger residents. Both the Playhouse and the community would contribute activities, with the former taking more of a back seat than had been the case for the October event.

However, in its realisation, the event proved to be a disappointment to both the centre and the Playhouse. On the day itself, a few activities were provided by the Playhouse, but the contribution that had been expected from the community was not forthcoming:

"We had a not too good event at Christmas, and that was a great learning event itself. For everyone concerned. For me it's about not consulting people widely enough, and misreading the expectations of people on the estate. Christmas parties in the past had been about the community centre giving out presents and not about jointly enjoying or celebrating something.

"The Christmas event was the one where we learnt. To be honest, a lot of it was outside pressure to say you've got to have a Christmas event. When we were trying to organise it there were one or two people who saw the success with the Playhouse and said, 'Oh they'll bring stuff.' We listened to other people instead of ourselves and got a bit greedy. We've learned now it's not just goods we can get but advice and help. Christmas was a big disappointment to us all. We sorted it out and it didn't affect the rest of the relationship."

Centre manager

One community member expressed the view that the Playhouse was "pissed off" with the failure of the community to deliver its part of the bargain as far as this event was concerned, and this may not have been a misreading of the initial reaction. However, it soon became clear to those involved that blame was not appropriate.

Actions speak louder than words, and that applies to the planning stage as well as delivery. A precedent had been established by the October event, when the Playhouse supplied virtually all of the activities as a way of introducing the project to the community. This proved to be a valid and successful strategy. However, it established an expectation on the part of the community that the Playhouse would provide the 'goodies'.

It seemed as if an instant dependency culture had been established, and the relative failure of the Christmas party illustrated this. Although the words exchanged in planning the second event presupposed a joint venture, the precedent was of a one-sided approach, and the precedent spoke louder than the words. The community were creating for themselves an extra workload in setting up the event, and the experience of someone else providing the event for them was simply too tempting:

"We'd been going down the road of being done to, by providers, and if we weren't very careful people come in to do all sorts of things and then go away again. Now its more about learning. I've learned how to say no to things that we can't do. Its given me confidence to say no we can't do that unless you give us the resources to do it."
Centre manager

After the high of the October event, there is no doubt that the Christmas event was an all-round disappointment, but it was also the catalyst for the most productive learning in the relationship. The bringing of gifts in October had been successful. Friendships and trust had been built. Punctuated by the Christmas event, a chapter of working together was about to begin.

chapter 7

Stage three: Theatre-going

Like most regional theatres, the West Yorkshire Playhouse mounts a family show each winter. Its annual offering is usually more lavish in production values, and runs for a longer period than is normal. Although it appeals to the regular theatre-goer, it is intended to appeal also to a wider, less regular audience. Past productions have been *Peter Pan, The Sound of Music,* and Gilbert and Sullivan's *Pirates of Penzance*, all of them having the capacity to appeal to a broad section of the community. The 1999 production was no exception – a stage version of the film musical *Singin' In The Rain*. Alongside it, in the smaller Courtyard Theatre, was a stage version of the perennial children's book favourite *Stig of The Dump*.

In 1996 the theatre had introduced a city-wide scheme to encourage community groups to attend theatre performances. Any bona fide tenants' association or community organisation in the inner city or outer council estates could make group bookings at very favourable rates. Until this point, no such bookings had been made by any groups from Ebor Gardens, but the Haslewood Tenants' Association, representing those living closest to the community centre, were very keen and they were prepared to open their doors to other residents as yet unformed into tenants groups. Their Chair had been closely involved in the Playhouse activities at the centre, and was keen to promote the ticket scheme to his members.

The timing was perfect. A new impetus was needed to overcome the sense of disappointment resulting from the Christmas Fair, and here were two productions that could easily be promoted to the members of the community. The older generations had been brought up with regular doses of *Singin' in the Rain* on film and television, and the children's production was also a relatively safe choice for those unused to attending theatre. As an introduction to attending the theatre, both productions were almost purpose-built.

Singin' in the Rain, one of the productions being performed at the Playhouse during the 'In our neighbourhoods' project, appealed to a broad range of residents.

Stig of the Dump proved particularly popular with younger residents. Reactions to visits to the Playhouse have been almost universally positive, and many residents spoke highly of their new-found activity.

So began an extraordinary and, for most people, surprising development in the relationship between the theatre and the community. Between December 1999 and July 2000, a total of over 200 tickets were sold to Ebor Gardens community group members. Many residents attended the theatre at least four times. Their selection of plays was eclectic and adventurous. They attended in groups of varying sizes, with a very wide age range, and with a large proportion of people attending as family groups.

Of all of the activities resulting from the 'In our neighbourhood' project, theatre attendances were regarded by the community as the most important. The ways in which residents value their newly-acquired access to the Playhouse are impressive and various:

"It means we can now go out and enjoy doing something we could never have afforded to do before. Which is really nice. It's a way of relaxing. We moved house a year ago and we had builders, plumbers, electricians, and then we were left with the decorating to do, and its lovely to go out and have a night away from it all. In a way you can sit at home and relax but you think, really we should be sanding the wall. I wouldn't go to the cinema because, I don't know, it's too flat. That sounds silly doesn't it? *[Laughs]* I don't watch television!"

It has been most fortuitous that a particular local opportunity for social activity has been 'discovered' at the very time that residents have felt confident enough to leave their homes unoccupied. Increased

The Ebor Gardens estate can at times feel alienating in scale. Physical regeneration encourages people to feel safer, but social regeneration also plays an important role in improving people's quality of life.

theatre attendance on this scale could not have come about without the refurbishment of the estate – as little as two years previously the project could not have had the same impact.

The reactions to the visits to the Playhouse have been almost universally positive, and interviewees have expressed no negative reactions to the plays themselves. One person with mobility problems expressed anxiety about the rake of the seating and difficulty reaching her seat, but her problem can be overcome now that the bookers know what to expect. Residents who went to the theatre felt comfortable in the environment, though several made it clear that they would only contemplate going as part of a group, which suggests that a degree of social insecurity might still exist without the support of friends.

Apart from the sheer pleasure of 'discovering' this new social outlet, other benefits were recognised as stemming from theatre attendances. Most significant was the growth of friendly relationships between residents:

"There's communication between people. They have lots of conversations about plays. I'm not saying they wouldn't talk to each other before, but now they say, 'Did you go and see such and such?' and have a bit of a discussion about what they thought about it. People start talking like that and then start talking about 'What we need to do on the estate is...' and, 'Wouldn't it be a good idea if...' and that's different. They have something in common to talk about."

This phenomenon cropped up in various places. The project manager for the refurbishment of Ebor

The 'In our neighbourhoods' project fortuitously occurred at the very time local people were feeling more confident about life on the estate. One result of the project was a shared interest and experiences.

Gardens has dealt with some fairly forceful tenants over the years, often complaining in community forum meetings about the inconveniences caused by the re-building process:

"I never thought I'd see the day when instead of talking about repairs and dog fouling, they're talking about the merits of one play against another. And these are people who never left their homes five or six years ago."

Activity at the community centre was stimulated by the growing habit of theatre-going. It is almost as if theatre tickets have become a form of window dressing for community activity:

"A lot of people come in here now, asking for tickets, and while they're here they say, 'What's this going on?' They're coming in here now instead of just wanting tickets, they're wanting to find out about what's on – 'Can we have a timetable, can we sign up for the computer course, can we do this and that?' We advertise the fact we're doing a theatre visit, people come in and say, 'Can anyone go?' It's getting like, 'Oh, we didn't know you did that', so we sign them up."

Resident

There is also evidence that residents are supportive to those who might be nervous of attending the theatre – "Come on, you come with us, it'll be fun!" As a result, families have created nights out for themselves, friends have attended with friends, wider acquaintances have been drawn in, and different generations have attended together. A local community activist, who took responsibility for initially organising the bookings, summed up the situation:

"I think people always thought of the Playhouse as very off-limits, a snobby, over priced place. They used to walk past saying, 'That's not for me, you'd have to dress up.' I think they now see it as somewhere afford-able, where people can go and have a night out with their family. It's not just one family now. People plan it about three or four weeks in advance – they save up for it. They'll go out a couple of hours before, take the kids to McDonalds or whatever, they have a drink, make a bit of a night of it. It's a very social thing now, something that was lacking on the estate.

"People used to be cooped up in their own little cages. They wanted to do something but were scared to leave their properties, and if they did leave they'd have nowhere to go, because people haven't got a lot of money; now they can.

"There's one or two people who have surprised me in that want to go to play after play after play. I thought it was just the novelty. Now they're asking, 'What's the special for Christmas?' And they're reading the little guides. 'Oh, there are press nights. Can we go to them? There's free wine and stuff!' And they're asking for the Heydays stuff that comes through the post. They want information now – before, they used to ignore information. Now they ask for it and pick out what they want to do."

The reference to planning is significant. Because of a sense of transience and insecurity on the estate, there was a tendency to avoid thinking too far into the future. The confidence to make plans, the avail-ability of a facility to plan for, and the ability to afford it, have all combined to make play-going a significant activity on the estate.

People to people

It may well be that, even with the above conditions in place, an uptake of tickets on such a scale would not have occurred without a significant level of familiarity with Playhouse personnel. One Playhouse staff member commented:

"Something has happened, and I think it must just be familiar faces. You tend to go to places that you feel comfortable about, and that's not just the architecture, or that you can work out where the café is; it's more about, 'Well, I know so and so, and they seem all right. So it must be OK.' And you come to something and think, 'That was really good, and I saw some people who looked like me there, so I might go again.'"

Part-time youth workers support after-school activities at the community centre.

45

Frequent visits to the community centre by staff from the Community and Education Unit led to first-name familiarity between the two groups. For Ebor Gardens residents 'the Playhouse' became a group of people rather than a building. For the Playhouse workers, 'Ebor Gardens' became a community rather than an estate. The familiarity started with joint planning of events, and the Playhouse providing certain activities. But gradually the relationship changed, accelerated by the Christmas experience.

It was the one-to-one involvement that emerged as most significant for the residents. Although the community and education staff had opened the doors, members of other departments soon became involved. Links between those booking theatre tickets and the box office have been widely praised, highlighting a great sense of welcome and inclusion from the staff:

> **"The box office staff have been very friendly and helpful. Other people have said that too. We're always very accepted. The tenants' groups now organise their own community network tickets without me. There are now six groups, and two more being formed, who have the community network forms. They're getting on with it without me, which is good."**
>
> *Resident*

Playhouse press and marketing staff have provided advice and expertise on setting up newsletters for the community, and the establishment of a web site for the centre. Although these services could have been secured from other sources, the 'style' of the Playhouse seems to have suited the community very well:

> **"There's been lots of little offshoots, like being able to go down there and ask advice and not being scared of getting a slap round the face or being seen as silly. Also we've got friends for life down there now. This thing *[In our neighbourhood]* runs out in September but we all feel confident enough now that we can go down if we've got a problem, and we can share things. If we need help in organising something we can go down and they can point us in the right direction. They've been organising things a lot longer than us – they've got the contacts too."**
>
> *Resident*

But the confidence about continuity is not entirely secure, and some community members are concerned that without a contact person at the Playhouse, the relationship could wither.

As well as its own permanent staff, the Playhouse engaged the services of two freelance arts workers to work with the community. One had a very open brief to explore possibilities with residents. Particularly effective engagement was with the members of The Lavender Group which comprises women wanting to be involved in sociable and creative activities, and with the luncheon club for elderly residents. She did not attempt to set up structured creative activity sessions with them, but instead worked with individuals, during their regular meetings, on personal writing. During the project she commented:

> **"The poetry from the luncheon club emerged from just having a chat. I raised**

The Lavender Group, which was in existence prior to the 'In our neighbourhood' project, worked with a writer from the Playhouse to express their experiences and hopes in a creative form.

the possibility, and they immediately said, 'Oh, we can't do poetry.' We just sat and talked, and as they spoke to me, I just wrote and then took it home. I then converted their words to poems and fed it back to them. Some of them said a lot, so it was easy to simply use their words. With others I had less to go on, so added bits. They are delighted. I've typed up copies for them, as well as for the exhibition on International Women Day. I'm getting their copies laminated too – one of them asked for a copy so she could put it up on her wall. They didn't want their names on them, but we will include a list of contributors. We did it again this morning with the women's group – we were going to do drama, but that was too scary."

An artist and writer who is also a resident on the estate, was also involved in creative writing sessions with groups that already existed. This contrasted with her work with a small group of young people, brought together to work on a mural on church property. Perhaps partly because this was a free-standing group, its activities gradually petered out. For several people on the estate, the general lack of engagement of the adolescent age group was a disappointment.

The reluctance to engage with more formal group creative sessions raises a number of issues. From the outset there had been expectations from both the Playhouse and the community workers that organised creative participation sessions would be a significant part of the developing programme of activities. This was backed up with requests for dance and drama sessions from residents who filled in a questionnaire issued by the community centre and the Playhouse.

Whether at the Playhouse or on the estate, new or already existing (such as Heydays), it was assumed that organised sessions would feature significantly. However, a dance session organised at the Playhouse for young people on Ebor Gardens attracted no takers; the suggested drama group has so far not materialised; none of the older residents on the estate chose to attend a Heydays taster session, despite the fact that some older residents had requested it. Even though confidence had been growing, there was still a reluctance to engage in more 'exposing' participatory activities. When asked to account for the success of the October event, the manager of the community centre said:

"The fun aspect – it wasn't pressurised. People felt they could just pop in and have a look. I'd been impressing that on the Playhouse people, that it needs to be low key and laid back, otherwise people here are frightened off."

This view would appear to be borne out, but there is still an expectation in some minds that such activities will eventually take off, that ideas need to be planted and given time to mature before they bear fruit. A gentle exposure to the unknown is required:

"[Before the improvements] Across the age groups people felt themselves in a walled castle – even now, they'll go to something if they know what it's about, but they're very nervous about participating, unless they know exactly what it's about."

Centre manager

Hence the success of the theatre visits, starting with a production where there were clear expectations, leading to more adventurous choices. There is every reason to assume that, with further reassurance and assistance, more challenging participatory activities could also become popular.

School involvement

Ebor Gardens Primary School, adjacent to the community centre, saw a growth in participatory activities as a result of the project. One of the Playhouse staff has been running drama sessions with younger pupils and their parents. She also organised craft sessions in which pupils made items for sale at the school Summer Fair. A party of Year Six pupils was taken on a tour of the backstage areas of the Playhouse, and the school welcomed a visit from the Schools Touring Company. Although the school had previously had a relationship with the Playhouse, it can be assumed that the increased take-up of Playhouse services is due to the presence on site of one of the staff from the theatre. The head teacher is very keen to continue to develop the relationship:

The Playhouse Children's Officer ran mask-making workshops at the school.

Following the workshops, a group of Year Six boys made papercraft items to sell at the school fair.

"The kids here are starved of first-hand experiences. It's important we have these links, especially as we're within walking distance."

The local secondary school, Agnes Stewart High School, also hosted a series of drama sessions for pupils experiencing behavioural difficulties.

Future developments

Although specific events have been organised by and with the Playhouse as part of the work with Ebor Gardens, none of the activities and services had been invented by the Playhouse for this project. Therefore, although the project had a life of only one year, there is no reason why the community should not continue to benefit from all that is on offer. The additional funding during the course of the year went largely on ensuring a presence on the estate, getting to know the residents and ensuring that information was getting through in an appropriate manner. Much of this was achieved by carrying out quite informal participatory activities within existing groups, and by providing one-to-one advice and support to key individuals on the estate. Such individuals are invaluable 'gatekeepers' in accessing the wider community; nurturing their involvement has been a key strategy in developing the relationship between the Playhouse and Ebor Gardens. A local council official who has been closely involved throughout the estate refurbishment process recognises the significance of such people:

"Agencies almost rely on 'professional tenants to get things done. The good ones are well-informed, work democratically and do a good job. The Playhouse directed most of its activities through the community centre, helped by one particular individual who encouraged people to get involved. Really, the jump in attendance was down to one or two people."

While this is true, a conscious effort has been made to increase the number of direct contacts, so that a sustained relationship, not over-dependent on too few individuals, can be achieved.

Part III

Analysis

chapter 8

Continuity and sustainability

Moving forward

Projects, initiatives, action research programmes... and all around, the everyday lives of people who will still be there well into the future. Attention to sustainability is always required, but rarely resourced, and as this project proceeded, the question 'What next?' arose in the minds of all concerned.

By January one deeply involved resident was expressing concerns about what would happen when the Rowntree project ended: he was concerned that the community might outstay its welcome, that staff at the Playhouse would no longer find the time to provide the support to which he had become accustomed. By May his attitude had changed:

> "We've got friends for life down there now. This thing runs out in September but we all feel confident enough now that we can go down if we've got a problem, and we can share things."

But that attitude could change again, and one therefore seeks some kind of assurance that any such anxiety is groundless. A project was undertaken in which appetites were whetted. Can they be satisfied?

Maintaining contact

The 'In our neighbourhood' project was predicated on the basis that the West Yorkshire Playhouse already had a range of established community services that could be promoted in the local community. The real issue was why those opportunities had not been grasped before by those who lived so close to the theatre. Although it was projected that some activities would be tailor-made for this project, much of the work was to be about encouraging uptake of existing possibilities. For example:

> "The tickets have been here all along, it's not like we've invented them. We didn't anticipate the project being a great proliferation of new events – we've already got lots on offer. If they come and don't like it, that's one thing, but if they are just not coming, why is that?"

The fact is that during the course of the project, play-going by Ebor Gardens residents rose from three in two years to at least 200 in eight months. Direct contact between individuals on the estate and staff at the Playhouse increased from none to a wide range of frequent and significant engagements. The local school became a regular user of the various Playhouse offerings and many residents became involved in creative activities led by Playhouse staff. None of these opportunities will cease at the end of the project. However, this is not to assume that the community will automatically continue to be involved.

Workers at the Playhouse and in the community all agree that the increased involvement was primarily due to face-to-face contacts, and the fact that people could identify with people rather than with institutions. No amount of written information was going to make a significant impact, whereas familiarity with a friendly face, initially on their own ground, generated a confidence among the residents to venture into the unfamiliar territory of the Playhouse.

The organisers of the various tenants' and residents' associations also benefited from personal contact with Playhouse staff, which encouraged them to promote ticket sales and to make use of advice and support from other, less familiar Playhouse personnel. These personal channels of communications have increased confidence and have been the conduit for information that might otherwise have been ignored.

It is also accepted by all parties, from both the community and the Playhouse, that maintaining such channels is fundamental to the continuing health of the relationship.

The involvement of many staff at the Playhouse will hopefully continue, but it may be wise to designate a particular point of contact for the future, as a safety net where other contacts are not so obvious. Maintaining the intensity of the contacts does have staffing implications, especially if the success of this project were to lead to a proliferation of similar projects with other communities: sustaining each new relationship would make a cumulative demand on existing staff, and might require additional posts.

In addition, there has been a clear demand from one of the groups at the centre for a continuation of the specialist art inputs supplied as part of this project. This input was made possible by the investment of the Joseph Rowntree Foundation, and it would clearly be a disappointment for the group concerned if no continuation could be supported from one source or another.

Resources

With the extraordinary uptake of theatre tickets under the Community Network scheme, it would be a tragedy if regular attendance by such a broad spectrum of residents could not continue. The much-praised services of the box office staff, the willingness of residents' association officers to organise theatre-going parties, and the ability of the Playhouse to offer tickets at the discounts available so far, will all be required into the future.

It is currently expected by the Playhouse that the concessionary rates can be maintained, even in the face of growing demand from across the city. This is largely because there is over-capacity in the first few days of each week, and the Community Network tickets will take up that capacity. As is the case with any ticket sales, demand will only be met when capacity allows, but one might foresee a situation in which Community Network groups are competing with full-price paying patrons – they might just get there first! Success may yet provoke a reappraisal of ticket pricing and marketing policies.

Replication

The Playhouse will be considering the potential of replicating this project with other communities in

Leeds. With the Community Network already well established, and being enthusiastically supported by many associations around the city, it may be appropriate to focus developmental activity on other areas in a rolling programme. Although the experience of this project would be invaluable, the specific features of this relationship do not create a precedent for other projects: the proximity of the estate to the Playhouse and the timely refurbishment of the physical environment of the estate made for a unique situation. Were a similar approach to be pursued elsewhere, a considerable strain could be put upon the existing staffing levels at the Playhouse.

However, the impact on this particular community, and the potential to have a similar impact elsewhere, once revealed cannot be ignored. One can only hope that with the additional funding projected both for education and for the regional repertory companies of the country, and with the current focus of the present government on social inclusion and community development, this project will be continued and replicated. Additional funding is always needed for any venture in the subsidised sector, and commitment and determination, and a creative use of existing staff time, can be enabled by such support. There are inevitable policy, financial and staffing implications in pursuing such a course, but the potential returns would appear to be very great.

chapter 9

What was valued?

Although this project was initiated by the West Yorkshire Playhouse, and only subsequently embraced by the local community, there has emerged a very clear sense of shared benefit.

Benefits to the Playhouse

In the early days, it may have seemed to some that the Playhouse was approaching the project in the role of benefactors. In the event, it is clear that the staff see themselves as having learned as much as the community, and made gains in a variety of ways. Having the chance to focus on one particular community, to get to know them in greater depth, and to acquire deeper insights into their aspirations has been very significant:

"It's made us more aware of what's going on. You have certain attitudes, about people and communities and what they do and don't want. In actual fact it's important to watch and listen and observe, and its quite different, what they want to what you think they want. Everybody's learnt a lot through this. Other departments have started to make links with the community as well. Quite often people can be a little bit narrow minded, and they just want to get on with what they've got to do, like marketing a product. But I think it's good that they see that we are a resource for the community. So it's not just about getting on with your

small part of the job, but opening up to the community and being there to help them if they need it."

The reference to the involvement of staff across the organisation is important, indicating that community relations are the responsibility of all Playhouse personnel: the knowledge and experience gained becomes applicable to all of the potential audiences and participants in the life of the Playhouse.

The project gave staff the time to reflect on the development of a relationship, to overcome small obstacles and to appreciate the need to take time in building relationships.

"I think we'd been providing up to Christmas, and when that went wrong we felt let down, but came to accept it. But things started to develop after Christmas – we learned that you've got to give it time to develop. We got used to making things happen very quickly, and that isn't always what is needed.

"I think it's changed the way we think about speed. We're used to organising activities and events and they are used to being the recipients of stuff. Its quite hard, because every time you construct some thing the ground gets pulled away underneath you, and you feel like it's your fault, but that's just the way it is. Some of them got down about that, and Christmas was quite debilitating, but our staff have different life experiences from the residents or staff there."

Playhouse project manager

That so many of the Playhouse staff contributed to the project, and that it was perceived to be successful by both sides, provided a different kind of return for the company:

"Members of staff in other departments have felt it was a great opportunity to do things they wouldn't otherwise have been able to do. They tend to be employed to do 'the thing', rather than work with other people. And I think people have entered a multitude of relationships. I think if it's perceived as a successful project, people will feel that's quite something, putting it alongside the achievement of having *Singin' in the Rain* at the National. If you can come out of this with good relationships with the community that's comparable with the other stuff. And it's more ongoing, and those people will always be there."

Playhouse project manager

Benefits to the community

Not surprisingly, the most frequently stated benefit for the community was that they were introduced to a good night out at the Playhouse, and for many, several good nights out. One senior citizen summed it up simply:

"We took 30 to 35 people from my end of the estate to *Singin' in the Rain* and *Visiting Mr Green*, and everyone thought it was

great. It gets people out and stops them having to sit on their own, so I think it's a good thing. I had thought it would be too high-price for working class people. Now I think it's good for everybody, designed and built to be accessible for everyone including the elderly and infirm."

The statement, from a very capable and active resident, illuminates the way in which the community has rallied round to enable others less active, and sometimes less confident, to use the facilities on offer. It would seem that an external focus, such as a theatre visit, can be a catalyst to nurture 'community spirit'.

Equally valued has been the access to advice and support on a one-to-one basis. The same resident commented:

"They've been very good coming in to give us advice and information with regard to setting up a newsletter. Which we very much appreciated. We had advice on costing, printing, presentation, ideas for contents. It worked as far as we were concerned. We intend to put something on for Christmas, so they might help with advice, costumes and so on."

Again the anticipation of future involvement is apparent. Such an approach could equally well have been explored by any other local business, offering its facilities and expertise, and there is no doubt that many such relationships do already exist. Whether there is any particular added impact derived from the fact that this particular business is theatre is debatable, but certainly the range of skills and techniques deployed in the successful running of a theatre lend themselves well to aspects of community development.

The project has apparently also had an effect on the running of the community centre in two particular ways. As indicated earlier, the ordering of theatre tickets at the community centre has encouraged residents to enquire about other activities offered by the centre. The project has also affected the way the community workers see their own activities:

"I've been here two years and my thinking has changed. The involvement we could have with the Playhouse hadn't occurred to me. It's highlighted the potential of what we could do. It's made more work for me. We've had some successful events and people want more. I'm trying to get some of the community to take stuff over. But much is batted back. I'm encouraging them – 'You can do this, take on responsibility.' But people need reassurance.

"Probably in many ways what I've found is what regeneration is, in terms of people. Are we doing 'to' people or 'with' people? I've looked at partnerships – much of what we used to do wasn't really partnerships as much as it could be."

Community worker

Playhouse staff were conscious of this extra pressure on the centre staff, and also of the fact that at the Playhouse they work as a team, providing each other with constant support and encouragement. Working constantly out in the community must at times seem like a lonely furrow to plough.

Communities are made up of individuals, and when the lives of a significant number of those individuals start to feel positive and enlivened, then the community starts to feel that way too. From their comments, it is clear that many residents have felt a sense of pleasure, of expectation for the future, and of greater social interaction. They have also experienced being included in a cultural activity that they may well have previously felt apart from. At this stage in the relationship it would be unwise to assume long-term and broader benefits, but it is clear that the community itself expects and intends a continuation of the access that they have enjoyed over the past year.

chapter 10

Theatre and community partnerships: some learning outcomes

As is doubtless the case with every theatre in the country, no one at the Playhouse consciously and deliberately put obstacles in the way of any sector of the community becoming involved with it. And yet for Ebor Gardens, as for so many parts of the country, a disproportionately low percentage of the residents was engaged with the theatre prior to this project.

No one had expected a significant increase in attendance at performances, but there had been hope of significant increases in creative activities promoted by the Playhouse. Things don't always turn out as expected, but whatever the intentions and eventual outcomes, a number of lessons have been learned about the process of developing such a relationship.

- ### Projects develop at their own pace
  Professional theatre companies are more used to deadlines than most organisations – if you've sold tickets for a first night, you'd better be ready for it! Consequently they become accustomed to making things happen fast. Community organisations tend to operate at a more organic pace, and Playhouse staff have sometimes had to accept a different timeframe to that which they are used to.

- ### Don't presume the needs and attitudes of local residents
  During this project, residents frequently surprised Playhouse staff with their interests and

concerns. It was a surprise to see the huge take-up of theatre tickets, and a surprise that there was relatively little take-up of the more participatory activities. Having the flexibility to respond to the demands of the community has been essential in making this project a success. It may well be that local communities elsewhere also want to partake in the mainstream cultural activities, if only they felt that they might be welcomed.

- ### Consult and listen
  This project was initially planned by the Playhouse, and only when the funding was secured was the community approached. This was effective in that it did not risk raising expectations without the certainty of delivery, but perhaps resulted in some early hiccups concerning ownership of the project. It was only with the increase in communication caused by the relative failure of one event, that the element of partnership in developing the relationship really took off.

- ### Work with existing groups rather than trying to create new ones
  By far the most successful aspects of the project have been those which have supplemented the work of existing groups. For example, ticket sales have flourished through the existing residents' and tenants' groups. Creative writing has emerged through the activities of the Lavender and luncheon club groups. Where the

Playhouse has attempted to set up groups with the aim of undertaking specific activities such as dance or drama, the response has been poor.

- *Don't expect instant participation; start with security*

By starting with tickets for a production that most people could relate to, and also by offering one-to-one support and advice, the relationship has been able to move towards more adventurous engagements. Once people became comfortable with the idea of attending the theatre, their choice of plays became more adventurous. Having explored creative writing in a very low-key way, alongside other activities, some groups are now contemplating more challenging activities such as a drama group. Probably the most reassuring factor has been getting to know various individuals from the Playhouse.

- *Relate to a number of residents*

Starting with a very small number of contacts in the community, the project has gradually expanded to the point at which a whole range of residents are taking on responsibility for liaising with the theatre. Instead of one person, seven now book tickets on behalf of residents. More are seeking advice from staff in different departments at the Playhouse. As is so often the case, it is essential to recognise the crucial role played by a small number of community activists, and widening that support base should be a central aim in all community development activities.

- *Give everyone a role in community relationships*

Although the Playhouse had originally intended to designate one member of staff to develop the relationship with Ebor Gardens, it soon became clear that the expertise and specialisms of a number of staff would be required. Initially it was the Arts Development team that had the most involvement, and while they remain the key contact point for the community, staff from the box office, marketing, development, catering and press departments have all become involved. This has made available a full range of expertise to the community, and created a greater sense of community commitment within the Playhouse.

chapter 11

Policy implications

It is not the place of this report to make policy recommendations to either the West Yorkshire Playhouse or the community of Ebor Gardens. However, the project has raised certain issues that may be of interest to policy makers both in the arts and in local government and community affairs.

Two aspects of the 'In our neighbourhood' project have proved to be extremely successful and highly valued by the community – cheap and accessible tickets for theatre performances; and access to professional support and advice from various Playhouse departments. The former has financial and staffing implications, and the latter has staffing implications only. **Should such benefits as these be actively promoted city-wide in Leeds, and be more vigorously promoted by other regional theatres, and if so, what policy decisions would be necessary to enable this?**

There is no doubt in the minds of both Playhouse and community workers that the increased face-to-face contact brought about during the project was a prerequisite for any successes during the year. Although costly in staffing time, the impact was far greater than any other medium of communication could have been in these circumstances. **If developing access to the theatre for local communities is a priority, what resource allocations would be appropriate in the future?**

The partnership between the Playhouse and the community, largely through the community centre and the local primary school, resulted in dialogues and a strengthened relationship, which in turn resulted in significant outputs in terms of community inclusion, and a range of specified outcomes for the community and the theatre. **To what extent can both the theatre, and those responsible locally for community development, capitalise on this experience in future partnership activities, for example through the newly formed Community Involvement Teams?**

chapter 12

Conclusions

In the introduction to this report we reproduce the aims and objectives of the 'In our neighbourhood' project. The project lasted for approximately 15 months, but the Ebor Gardens Estate and West Yorkshire Playhouse expect to be neighbours for a number of decades to come. The overarching aim, 'To generate a productive and sustainable relationship between the community of Ebor Gardens and the West Yorkshire Playhouse', is therefore to be seen in two parts, the first being the generation of the relationship, and the second being the sustainability of the relationship.

The range of engagements between the two parties, and the evident satisfaction with those engagements, would clearly indicate that a productive relationship has been generated. Its nature provided some surprises all round, both in terms of the most successful activities and the outcomes resulting from those activities. While the extent of the relationship could of course have been greater, encompassing even more of the community, the level of satisfaction with the project was generally very high.

To draw any conclusions about the sustainability of the project would be premature. At certain times, concerns were expressed on the part of the community that the intensity of the relationship might fade, and there is no doubt that all parties are conscious of the need to continue to nurture the relationship. This can be achieved in the context of the ongoing services provided by the West Yorkshire Playhouse to community groups around Leeds. Indeed, although the first objective of the project was 'Over the course of a year, to increase the range and quality of what the Playhouse offers the community', much of what took place was already in existence. Certainly some activities, such as the celebratory events, placing artists in the community to generate creative activities, and one-to-one advice on a variety of issues, were generated for this project alone.

But most of the growth in activity fell under the second objective, 'to increase the take-up by the community of new and existing WYP services and products, through improved accessibility'. Ticket sales through Community Network, the costume hire department, advice from staff in different departments, backstage tours and school tours all saw increased take-up during the year, but all had been available before the project began. (Only Heydays, the weekly creative activities sessions for older people, failed to attract additional members through this project; but then Ebor Gardens community centre has its own thriving provision for the elderly.) It is agreed by all that the energy put into placing Playhouse staff in the community during the project was the crucial factor in increasing the take-up.

Those contacts, led by the Arts Development Unit, stimulated activity in realising the third objective, 'To increase the awareness and commitment of the whole WYP institution and its staff to supporting the needs and aspirations of the local community.' The experience and insights thus gained by the Playhouse staff should prove invaluable in developing similar relationships across the city. For example, the marketing department may wish to consider the effect on ticket sales of staff spending time in the community.

However, it will always be necessary for the staff to balance their time in fulfilling their own specialist functions within the organisation, and contributing to relations with the community. It is the fact that the Playhouse is a theatre-producing institution that makes it a valuable community resource, and only if the primary function is properly attended to can its value to the community be realised.

It would appear that certain preconceptions about community needs and interests have been challenged. It might even be argued that there was a presumption that this community would not be particularly interested in theatre-going, and that the focus should be on creating more community orientated activities for them. In the event, the number of theatre attendances and the uptake of support and advice clearly indicate that a theatre can be a really significant resource for its local community, whatever the overall aspirations of the theatre.

There need be no conflict between a regional, national and international profile and a local significance. Indeed, the health of the organisation, which enables it to fulfil its wider ambitions, may well be nurtured by its local involvement. Balancing the resources between these different aspects of the organisation's operations requires attention and commitment, but can be justified on wider grounds than social conscience or window-dressing for funders.

The fact that the project was the subject of research and reporting seems to have resulted in a more conscious consideration of the issues being raised. Although this may at times have created a different aspect of stress, it was agreed to have been valuable to the process itself, and to the potential for future work by the Playhouse:

"It did create extra pressure because the outcomes are going to be serious-minded and significant. It's made us look for the relevance and significance in everything we do. And being evaluated like this is new to us. It will feel like a help afterwards, whatever the pressure during the process."

Playhouse staff

Being interviewed as part of the process seems to have had its own impact on the residents of Ebor Gardens as well:

"It's given permission for people to say more. What I feel is that people are dying to give their opinions about things. It's opened the floodgates. It's made me think, you make all sorts of assumptions – but did I ask them? No, I didn't. I suppose it's affected the process. For years people mistakenly fed stuff to them – what's good for them. Now people feel they can say exactly what they feel. You don't have to dress it up."

Centre manager

And so back to the question of sustainability, now that the 'In our neighbourhood' project itself has finished. The neighbours have developed a bit of a habit of dropping in on each other. With continued attention to each other's needs and interests, there is no reason to suppose that the habit will cease. A community that was previously not using the services of its most adjacent cultural resource, is now regarding the place as theirs, that, to use the words of the Chief Executive of the Playhouse, "the theatre is a club of which everyone can consider themselves to be a member." To lead a fulfilling life, human beings need a sense of future, and planning a good night out contributes to that sense.

Before this project, no one was excluding the residents of Ebor Gardens from the Playhouse. It might even be said that the residents were excluding themselves, but there is very little distinction between being excluded and excluding oneself. Through various channels, the Playhouse had always been inviting the widest range of people to use its facilities, but as the saying goes, 'If they didn't hear it, you didn't say it.'

It took a sustained effort to make direct contact with the residents, to ensure that they had all the information they needed, before they felt that they too could use the Playhouse. If the nearest neighbours hadn't been hearing, then what about everyone else? And does it matter if some don't hear? The West Yorkshire Playhouse is a notably successful organisation: like many other cultural institutions, it could continue to flourish with the support of only those who expect, and are

expected, to engage with the arts. But is that enough? It has been estimated that less than a quarter of the population engage regularly with the subsidised arts. Perhaps it's time for the silent majority to find their voice and to take their seats. From the Chief Executive again:

"The arts are being besieged by demands for the measurement of their impact on the lives of local people. But it is equally important to measure the impact a community has on an arts organisation, and the style in which it manages its work. The central message of this research is that, as with everything else in life, personal relationships need to be developed and embedded in working practice before partnerships can develop in a balanced, purposeful and unpatronising way."

Perceptions of exclusion are as real as actual exclusion, and overcoming them is the responsibility of all parties. We all have preconceptions and prejudices about our place and other peoples' places in this world, and only by going out to make relationships can we overcome them.

We start in our neighbourhood, and then....?

West Yorkshire Playhouse

In our neighbourhood – Developing potential through the arts

Background

The West Yorkshire Playhouse has a reputation for innovation, not just in its productions but significantly in its community and education programme. This new project provides an opportunity for the organisation to create, develop and consolidate a sophisticated set of relationships with the Ebor Gardens area of Leeds whose residents are struggling with a range of problems associated with low educational achievement, unemployment and a range of socio-economic issues.

Ebor Gardens is an inner city community cut off from the city centre by busy roads, including the inner city motorway. Housing improvements are being undertaken as part of an SRB Project. However, the estate and those adjacent to it house some of the poorest and isolated members of society. Some of the housing stock is still in a poor condition, used only for housing homeless people, single parents, those sections of the community dependent on state support in many forms.

There are two secondary schools serving the area, one has recently had an OFSTED inspection which determined that it was suffering 'serious weakness'. The local primary school is waiting to be rebuilt.

There are agencies, both voluntary and state sector, at work in the area, particularly in the school and with parents who need encouragement and support to help them work with their children on key skills, literacy and numeracy. Geographically this area is adjacent to the Playhouse, with only the inner city motorway fly-over separating us. A number of discreet projects have taken place over the nine years that the Playhouse has been open, including:

- Support for the local drama group from creative staff at the Playhouse, director, musical director, stage management and carpenters.
- Activities with children from the primary school both in school and at the Playhouse, focused on creative themes and skills.
- Curriculum-based projects with the secondary school involving Year Nine pupils, looking at a production from rehearsal to press night, meeting actors, director, designer, sitting in on rehearsals and talking to actors about reviews.

It is the success of these individual projects which leads us to believe that a concerted piece of work with this geographical area would provide a beneficial project.

The success and reputation of the Playhouse's community and education work has been founded on the building of successful relationships with other agencies, both local and national. Our philosophy is one which is inclusive and visionary, one which draws organisations together on mutual territory allowing unusual and creative initiatives to flourish. The project we anticipate undertaking in our local community will draw support from Leeds TEC, Leeds City Council and Leeds Metropolitan University amongst others. But the project will be a demonstration of how one organisation can create a diversity of relationships enabling a community with low expectations for education and employment to find a way out.

Aims

The overarching aim of the project is to create an innovative model for a relationship between an arts institution and a neighbourhood which is struggling with social and economic problems, in the context of a strategic moment for arts policy nationally. This will be done by:

- Providing a dedicated member of staff to facilitate what we have to offer our local community.
- Improving the quality of what we offer our local community.
- Improving access to the West Yorkshire Playhouse for a deprived community through appropriate targeting.

Policy relevance

Nationally, the Department of Culture, Media and Sport (DCMS), through its Minister Chris Smith, is currently very keen to address the issue of audience development and access. Arts and sports organisations will ensure pricing structures do not exclude young people or those who do not currently attend

such activities. However, we are keen to stress that there is more to this issue than purely pricing.

The Playhouse's artistic policy stresses the importance of engagement with the community in an active and participative way. Not looking for a passive relationship, but one which goes to the heart of empowering people to develop their own artistic skills from the philosophical position that everyone can be an artist.

The moment is right for providing a quality national model which encourages real debate about policies operated by organisations, ensuring there is not a cynical response from arts organisations to the DCMS just to gain funding. Jude Kelly, Artistic Director of the West Yorkshire Playhouse, is the Vice Chair of the National Advisors Committee for Creative and Cultural Education, so communication channels are open.

Methods

The Playhouse will undertake a programme of community development initiatives including face-to-face contact work which will facilitate local people's involvement in our existing community and education programme.

The Development Worker will provide information to local groups and act as a broker for the development of new relationships with other organisations and agencies in the city.

These include the Under-Eights Service, Leeds Metropolitan University, National Childminders' Association, and other arts organisations in Leeds.

It may be that new events are organised to provide an appropriate method of engagement with a particular group which will inform our longer term development, and there are a huge range of already existing Playhouse projects which we can access to provide arts education opportunities for the community.

The 'In our neighbourhood' project will provide a vital piece of research and establish a pattern for community use and developing a long-term relationship, which could be a model for other institutions.

The following case studies illustrate the potential for community groups' engagement with existing projects:

1 Arts Alive

A project grown from local demand for access to training for those working with pre-school aged children. Arts activity has been identified as a way of encouraging younger children's understanding of the world. However, most organisations providing care for younger children cannot afford to pay for artists. The next-best thing is for staff to acquire skills in arts activities. Arts Alive, run by the Playhouse, takes place on a Saturday morning twice each term and provides a broad programme of quality arts inputs from professionals. Sessions have included dance and movement, drama, making musical instruments, story making, using books, making and using puppets, plus a series of theoretical inputs from Leeds Metropolitan University on how children learn, and the importance and relevance of play.

Those participating in Arts Alive are individual childminders, playgroup staff from the voluntary sector, early-years centre staff from the state sector and parents and volunteers from nurseries and mother-and-toddler groups.

This project has been established as a model of accessibility and would be the ideal opportunity for local parents and those caring for young children to get involved. Partners involved in Arts Alive are: the National Association of Childminders, Leeds Metropolitan University and Leeds City Council's Under-Eights Service. This diversity of partners illustrates the potential for individuals involved.

2 Spark –
Sport and Arts towards Knowledge

The Playhouse has developed the SPARK project over the last year with the support of Leeds United Football Club, Leeds Rhinos Rugby League, Leeds Education Authority and Leisure Services.

The Playhouse creates a programme of activities which take place in inner city after-school clubs and community centres. Some of the activity is sport and some arts. The purpose is to encourage children's learning outside school time and provide them with stimulating activity. SPARK has attracted funding from the commercial sector (Provident Financial), from the Foundation for Sport and the Arts and the Gulbenkian Foundation. Leeds TEC have funded an additional element which is a training programme for voluntary and paid sessional workers. This programme, *SPARK EXTRA*, provides practical ideas for activities which staff can take away from each session, plus contacts from supportive organisations. The University of Leeds School of Continuing Education also offer sessions covering subjects to do with child development, child protection and special issues regarding children in care.

Local people could access this project and gain support from agencies involved, thus improving the quality of after-school provision for children and providing training opportunities for staff.

April 1999 – March 2000

April 1999	Mapping of local groups and initial contacts.
May/June/July	In-depth discussion with groups to begin facilitation of access to Playhouse projects – meetings between group leaders and Playhouse staff to investigate potential.
August	Special summer activity programme – one-off projects.
September	Review of project to date, taster sessions planned and undertaken, focusing on education initiatives and linking to our existing projects.
October/ November	Planning for celebratory event begins.
December	Access to existing projects continues.
January/ February 2000	Celebratory community event – 10 years of WYP and Millennium.
February/March	Review of project activity and gathering of information to use as a model for other cities/regions.

Staffing

Through this project we would look to employ a development worker who would be the physical contact point between the Playhouse and the local area.

Other members of the Arts Development Unit would be involved in the project, helping to draw in potential from the neighbourhood, advise on how relationships could develop through existing projects and undertake specific new events.

The Playhouse has developed a style of working which enables development of innovative work which is then reviewed and modified before being consolidated into core working practice.

The total cost of the project will be £25,017.00.

Evaluation/dissemination

The success of a project such as this would be quantified in a range of ways.

We would look to see an increase in the number of relationships we had developed both with individuals and groups from the area. Also:

a. How groups and key community figures had

used Playhouse events and activities to enhance the experiences of local people.

b. How much the arts feature in programmes offered by community groups before and after the period of this project.

c. Examine the educational development of individuals in the community, looking at connections made into higher education and further education.

d. Look at the diversity of relationships each group has developed with Playhouse departments, e.g. links to box office, carpenters, stage management, education department and wardrobe department.

Evidence of these relationships developed will provide a picture of a range of threads which, combined, will illustrate a complex web of connections illustrating how an arts organisation can support arts, educational and social development in communities.

Information on the development of this project would be available to other arts organisations through producing articles in appropriate publications and working with arts funding bodies – the Arts Council of England and regional arts bodies.

As mentioned in 'Policy relevance' above, we will be discussing the project with the DCMS.

Other support

If our proposal does not fulfil the Joseph Rowntree Foundation's Current Priorities it will be a missed opportunity to create an innovative model of the interface between communities and arts institu-

tions at this strategically important time. The cost of this project is small compared to its potential to influence national arts funding policy and community development in other areas of the UK. It would be difficult to attract funding for this type of project from other sources.

Summary

'In our neighbourhood' is a project which will provide an innovative approach for arts organisations to develop relationships with their local communities.

The Playhouse will act as a 'hub' in a sophisticated set of relationships between institutions in the city, community groups and schools in the area. Using the arts as 'oil' in a regeneration programme, community groups, key individuals, school staff and pupils will be drawn into a relationship with the Playhouse through a range of projects which in turn will lead to discreet relationships with other institutions.

The purpose of the project is to provide a community with:

- The means to make use of community assets, e.g. Playhouse, University, etc.
- Access opportunities in education and training.
- Ways of seeing the arts as an end in themselves as well as a tool to acquiring confidence and skills.

The Playhouse has a wide-reaching portfolio of projects, relationships and opportunities for groups. 'In our neighbourhood' aims to draw local people into a long-term developmental relationship which could be replicable in other cities as an example of community learning. The Playhouse represents an organisation taking responsibility for providing the communities in its neighbourhood with ways into a wider world. The complexity of these relationships is illustrated more fully in the diagram below.

We propose to appoint a dedicated member of staff to facilitate what we have to offer our local community and, through appropriate targeting, to improve access for a deprived community.

In our neighbourhood: developing potential through the arts

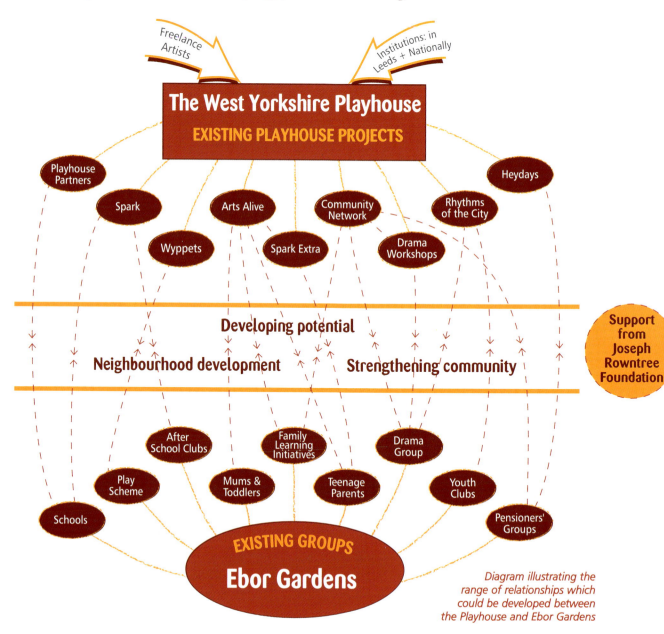

Diagram illustrating the range of relationships which could be developed between the Playhouse and Ebor Gardens

The research on which this report is based proceeded throughout the life of the 'In our neighbourhood' project. The research was designed to be integrated into the project, rather than existing as an objective outsider view.

By far the greatest part of the research was done via interviews with participants both within the Playhouse staff, and in the community of the Ebor Gardens Estate. In all, over 35 interviews were conducted, most on a one-to-one basis, but several involving a group. These interviews, many transcribed from tape recordings, are quoted extensively in the report, but the interviewees remain anonymous.

Documentary research also took place, including Playhouse policy documents and a 1991 report commissioned by Leeds City Council from housing consultants Chapman Hendy, on the condition of the Ebor Gardens Estate at that time.

All analysis and interpretation of the evidence gleaned from the interviewees is the responsibility of the researcher. However, the intention has been to reflect as accurately as possible the perspectives of the participants, and with this in mind they were given the opportunity to respond to the draft of the report.

The project was unique in that it was 'location specific' but there are elements of relevance for other arts and community situations. The account sets out to share lessons and insights gained rather than claim any 'models of good practice'.

Notes

1 See proposal from WYP to JRF, appendix A.

2 Of the total entries of 140,000, it is estimated that around 40,000 are 'active'. On a pro rata basis, one might therefore estimate that only 2 or 3 Ebor Gardens residents are active users of the Theatre.

3 Heydays is a weekly gathering of people over 55 for creative activities.

4 Jude Kelly, artistic director WYP, in presentation to Adult Education class, 1994.

5 These points have been listed from interviews with professional and voluntary social workers, teachers and residents.

6 Estate Strategy and Associated Action Bid Sept 1991 Chapman Hendy Assocs Ltd, Housing Consultants, Leeds.